Jesus on the Sea

KEVIN MAYHEW LTD
Rattlesden Bury St Edmunds
Suffolk England
IP30 0SZ

OPENBOOK PUBLISHERS
205 Halifax Street
Adelaide
SA 5000
Australia

ISBN 0 86209 428 3

Printed in Great Britain

Jesus on the Sea

Retold from Scripture by Susan Sayers
and illustrated by Arthur Baker

Kevin Mayhew

In Israel there is a big lake called the Sea of Galilee. It is a very beautiful place set among the hills with clear, fresh water. Mostly it is very calm and quiet. But sometimes it isn't a bit calm. Sudden winds whip up the water to a wild excitement. And when that happens, wise fishermen head for home!

Jesus knew the lake well; some of his best friends were fishermen. He had met Peter and Andrew, James and John while they were busy mending their nets.

'Peter,' said Jesus one warm evening, 'can we sail over to the other side today?' 'Yes, of course, Lord,' said Peter. 'Hop in.'

Jesus climbed aboard and sat down amidships. James and John pushed the strong boat out, before leaping in themselves. Andrew hoisted the sail and Peter took the helm.

Jesus was tired after being awake since well before dawn. He had also climbed up into the quiet hills to pray. The sun glinted on the water, and a light breeze gently rocked them to and fro. It wasn't long before Jesus nodded off to sleep.

Suddenly, out of nowhere, a fierce wind blew up. The sea churned and boiled angrily, and the boat rolled and tossed on the waves, up and down, up and down. One wave crashed right into the boat, and James and Andrew had to bale out water as fast as they could.

'Reef the sail!' 'Turn her into the wind!' 'Bail faster!' Everyone was shouting. James looked across at Jesus. 'Good gracious!' he thought, 'Jesus is still asleep!'

'WAKE UP, JESUS, WAKE UP!
We're in danger of drowning,
and we need your help!'

Jesus didn't seem bothered by the weather. But he looked lovingly at their anxious faces and stood up in the prow of the boat. In a firm, calm voice he spoke to the raging sea. 'Be still!' ordered Jesus.

Straight away the wind started to relax, and became gentle again. The sea settled down and lapped quietly round the boat. The lake was once more at peace.

The fishermen were amazed. ‘Who on earth can this man be?’ they asked each other. ‘Even the wind and waves obey him.’

Another time, after Jesus had spent all day healing and teaching in the hills, he sent his friends on ahead in the boat. He went off on his own to pray.

He could see them out on the lake, battling against a strong wind.

Jesus started to walk out to them, walking on the water. When they saw him, they got quite scared. 'It's . . . it's . . . a g-g-g . . . ghost!' cried Andrew. He had never seen anyone walking on water before. 'Don't be afraid,' called Jesus, waving to them, 'it's only me!'

Peter wasn't so sure. 'If it really is you,' he said, 'let me come and walk to you on the water.' Jesus smiled. 'Come on, then,' he answered. Peter climbed out of the boat rather gingerly, looking at Jesus all the time. It was amazing – he found himself walking on the sea!

Then he started to panic. 'Supposing I sink,' he thought nervously. Sure enough, he started to drop down into the water.

‘Help!’ shouted Peter. ‘Help! I’m drowning!’ Quick as a flash, Jesus’ strong arms were there to hold him and pull him out. Together they went back to the boat and climbed in.

'You didn't trust me enough, you see,' Jesus told Peter. 'That's why you started to sink.' Strangely enough, now that Jesus was with them, the wind seemed friendly again. They reached the other side of the lake in no time.

Soon the Sea of Galilee was silent and empty again, calm and peaceful under the stars. It seemed contented and happy. Perhaps it knew that Jesus was God – and, after all, it was God who made the wind and the sea.

Note for parents:
This story can be found in the Gospel of Mark, chapters 4 and 6, and in the Gospel of John, chapter 6.